Dear Parents and Educators,

Welcome to Puffin Young Readers! As parents
know that each child develops at his or her ow~
speech, critical thinking, and, of course, readin~
Readers recognizes this fact. As a result, each P~ ~~ders
book is assigned a traditional easy-to-read level (~ ~) as well as a
Guided Reading Level (A–P). Both of these systems will help you choose
the right book for your child. Please refer to the back of each book for
specific leveling information. Puffin Young Readers features esteemed
authors and illustrators, stories about favorite characters, fascinating
nonfiction, and more!

Young Cam Jansen and the Missing Cookie

LEVEL 3

GUIDED READING LEVEL **J**

This book is perfect for a **Transitional Reader** who:
- can read multisyllable and compound words;
- can read words with prefixes and suffixes;
- is able to identify story elements (beginning, middle, end, plot, setting, characters, problem, solution); and
- can understand different points of view.

Here are some **activities** you can do during and after reading this book:
- Descriptive Words: The author of this book uses lots of descriptive words. For example, instead of writing "lots of hairs on your sleeve," he writes "lots of *short, white* hairs on your *right* sleeve." Reread the story and try to find as many descriptive words as you can. Try to read some of the sentences without the descriptive words. Which do you think sounds better?
- Compound Words: A compound word is made when two words are joined together to form a new word. Look for the following compound words in the story: birthday, chalkboard, homework, lunchroom, notebook, something. On a separate piece of paper, write down the definition of each compound word. Then break each word into two separate words and write down the meaning of those words.

Remember, sharing the love of reading with a child is the best gift
you can give!

—Bonnie Bader, EdM
    Puffin Young Readers program

*Puffin Young Readers are leveled by independent reviewers applying the standards developed by Irene Fountas and Gay Su Pinnell in *Matching Books to Readers: Using Leveled Books in Guided Reading*, Heinemann, 1999.

For teachers everywhere who introduce our
children to the magic of reading—DA

For Amanda—SN

Puffin Young Readers
Published by the Penguin Group
Penguin Group (USA) Inc., 375 Hudson Street, New York, New York 10014, USA
Penguin Group (Canada), 90 Eglinton Avenue East, Suite 700, Toronto, Ontario M4P 2Y3, Canada
(a division of Pearson Penguin Canada Inc.)
Penguin Books Ltd., 80 Strand, London WC2R 0RL, England
Penguin Group Ireland, 25 St. Stephen's Green, Dublin 2, Ireland (a division of Penguin Books Ltd.)
Penguin Group (Australia), 250 Camberwell Road, Camberwell, Victoria 3124, Australia
(a division of Pearson Australia Group Pty. Ltd.)
Penguin Books India Pvt. Ltd., 11 Community Centre, Panchsheel Park, New Delhi—110 017, India
Penguin Group (NZ), 67 Apollo Drive, Rosedale, Auckland 0632, New Zealand
(a division of Pearson New Zealand Ltd.)
Penguin Books (South Africa) (Pty.) Ltd., 24 Sturdee Avenue,
Rosebank, Johannesburg 2196, South Africa

Penguin Books Ltd., Registered Offices: 80 Strand, London WC2R 0RL, England

Text copyright © 1996 by David A. Adler. Illustrations copyright © 1996 by Susanna Natti. All rights
reserved. First published in 1996 by Viking and in 1998 by Puffin Books, imprints of Penguin Group
(USA) Inc. Published in 2011 by Puffin Young Readers, an imprint of Penguin Group (USA) Inc.,
345 Hudson Street, New York, New York 10014. Manufactured in China.

The Library of Congress has cataloged the Viking edition
under the following Control Number: 95046462

ISBN 978-0-448-45823-6   10 9 8 7 6 5 4 3

Young Cam Jansen
and the Missing Cookie

by David A. Adler

illustrated by Susanna Natti

Puffin Young Readers
An Imprint of Penguin Group (USA) Inc.

Contents

Chapter 1
Click!

Rrrr!

The school bell rang.

It was time for lunch.

Mrs. Dee told the class,

"Don't go yet.

First copy your homework."

Mrs. Dee wrote six math problems

on the chalkboard.

The children in the class copied them.

But not Cam Jansen.

Cam looked at the board.

She closed her eyes and said, "Click!"

Cam always closes her eyes

and says "Click!" when she wants

to remember something.

Then Cam opened her eyes.

She waited for her friend Eric Shelton.

He was copying the homework.

When he was done,

Cam and Eric went to the lunchroom.

Jason Jones sat with Cam and Eric.

Jason said to Cam,

"You didn't copy the homework."

Cam smiled.

"I don't need to copy it," Cam said.
"I remember it."

Jason said, "No one can remember all those numbers."

Eric said, "Oh, yes.

Cam has an amazing memory."

Cam closed her eyes and said, "Click!"

Then she read off all the numbers.

"So what!" Jason said.

"I didn't bring my notebook.

Maybe those are the wrong numbers."

Cam's eyes were still closed.

She said, "Click" again.

"Jason," she said,

"you're wearing a polka-dot shirt.

There are seven polka dots

on your shirt pocket."

Jason counted the dots on his pocket.

Cam was right.

"And there are lots of short, white hairs on your right sleeve."

"Those are Emily's hairs," Jason said.

"She's my dog.

I played with her this morning."

Jason brushed off some of the hairs.

Then he said,

"You didn't remember all that.

You were peeking.

I'll prove it."

Cam's eyes were still closed.

Jason took a piece of paper

from his pocket.

He wrote, "Say yes

if you want a chocolate chip cookie."

Jason held the paper in front of Cam.

She didn't say yes.

But Eric said yes.

"No," Jason told him.

"I wrote this only for Cam.

And if she didn't say yes

to a chocolate chip cookie,

maybe she's not peeking.

Maybe she really does have

an amazing memory."

Chapter 2
The Missing Cookie

Cam opened her eyes.

"My memory is like a camera,"
Cam said.

"I have a picture in my head
of everything I've seen.
'Click!' is the sound my camera makes
when it takes a picture."

Cam's real name is Jennifer.

But because of her great memory,
people started to call her
"the Camera."

Then "the Camera" became just Cam.

Cam took a cheese sandwich

out of her lunch bag.

Eric took out a jelly sandwich.

Jason opened his lunch box.

He took out an egg salad sandwich.

"Hey!" Jason said.

"Where is my chocolate chip cookie?"

Cam and Eric looked
into Jason's lunch box.
There were cookie crumbs inside it.
But no cookie.
Jason said, "Last night
I put the cookie in my lunch box.
Now it's gone.
Someone stole my chocolate
chip cookie."

Chapter 3
Stop Him!

"But who would steal a cookie?"
Cam asked.

Jason said, "During class
my lunch box was in the closet.
Anyone could have opened it.
Maybe Pam took the cookie.
She sits near the closet.
For lunch she only gets
a sandwich and carrot sticks."

Eric shook his head.

"It wasn't Pam," he said.

"I baked sugar cookies,
and I gave her one.
But she wouldn't eat it.
She doesn't like cookies."

Cam said, "Your sugar cookies
were burned.
That's why she didn't want one."

Jason looked around the lunchroom.

"Look at Susie," he said.

Susie was eating a big, round cookie.

"That may be my cookie."

Susie was at the other end of the room.

Jason walked over to her.

Cam said to Eric,

"I don't think Susie would steal."

Cam bit into her sandwich.

She sipped her milk and thought.

Jason came back to the table.

"Susie was eating an oatmeal

cookie," he said.

"She baked it herself."

Cam ate some more of her sandwich.

A few crumbs dropped onto the table.

Eric told Jason, "Lots of people

have big cookies for lunch."

"Not like mine," Jason said.

"My dad made it.

It has lots and lots of chocolate chips."

Cam looked at the sandwich crumbs

that were on the table.

Then she closed her eyes

and said, "Click!"

She wanted to remember something.

Jason looked at the next table.

He saw Annie take a big cookie

from her lunch box.

Jason said, "Look at all the chocolate

chips in that cookie.

That's the cookie Dad baked for me."

Jason ran to Annie's table.

Cam opened her eyes.

"Stop him!" Cam said.

"Annie didn't take his cookie.

But I know who did."

Chapter 4
The Thief

It was too late to stop Jason.

He was already at Annie's table.

Cam dropped her sandwich.

She ran to Annie's table.

Eric followed her.

Annie was about to eat

the chocolate chip cookie.

Cam, Eric, and Jason
were looking at Annie.
Other children were looking, too.
"My birthday is tomorrow,"
Annie said.
"Are you here to surprise me?
That's so nice."
"I'm not here to be nice," Jason said.

"Stop!" Cam said.

"I know who took your cookie."

"I know, too," Jason said.

"Annie took it!"

Annie looked at her cookie.

Then she said, "I took this from home.

It's mine!"

Annie bit into her chocolate

chip cookie.

Cookie crumbs fell onto the table.

"Annie is right," Cam said.

"It *is* her cookie."

Cam looked inside Annie's lunch box.

She told Eric and Jason

to look inside Annie's lunch box, too.

"It's empty," they said.

Cam said, "Now let's look

in Jason's lunch box."

Cam, Eric, and Jason

went back to their table.

They looked in Jason's lunch box.

"It's empty, too," Eric said.

"No, it's not," Cam said.

She turned the lunch box upside down.

Crumbs fell onto the table.

"You had crumbs in there
because your cookie was eaten
while it was still *inside*
your lunch box."

"Who would eat a cookie that way?"
Jason asked.

Cam pointed to the short, white hairs
on Jason's sleeve and said,

"A dog would eat a cookie that way!"

"Of course," Jason said.

"It was Emily.

She ate my cookie.

She'll eat anything."

Cam, Eric, and Jason

finished eating their sandwiches.

Then Eric said to Jason,

"I'm sorry your cookie is gone.

You can have some of mine."

Eric gave Jason two sugar cookies.

"Thank you," said Jason.

He looked at the cookies.

He gave them back to Eric.

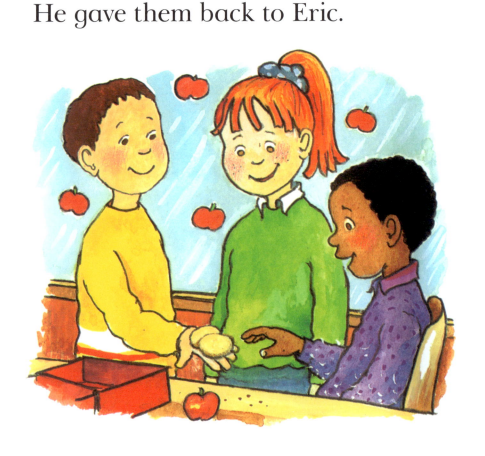

"You are a good friend," Jason said.

"But you are not a good baker.

Cam was right.

Your sugar cookies are burned.

Even Emily wouldn't eat them."

"Well, I would," Eric said.

And he did.

A Cam Jansen Memory Game

Take another look at the picture on page 6.
Study it.
Blink your eyes and say, **"Click!"**
Then turn back to this page
and answer these questions:

1. Are Cam's eyes open or closed?

2. What color is Cam's shirt?

3. How many children are there
   in the picture?

4. Is Cam's notebook open or closed?

5. Is that a pen or a pencil
   on Cam's notebook?